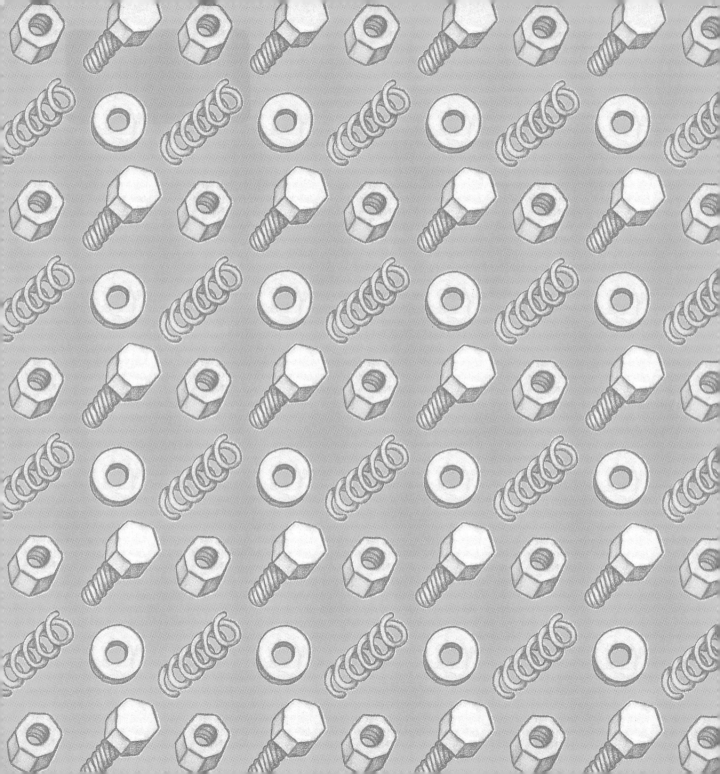

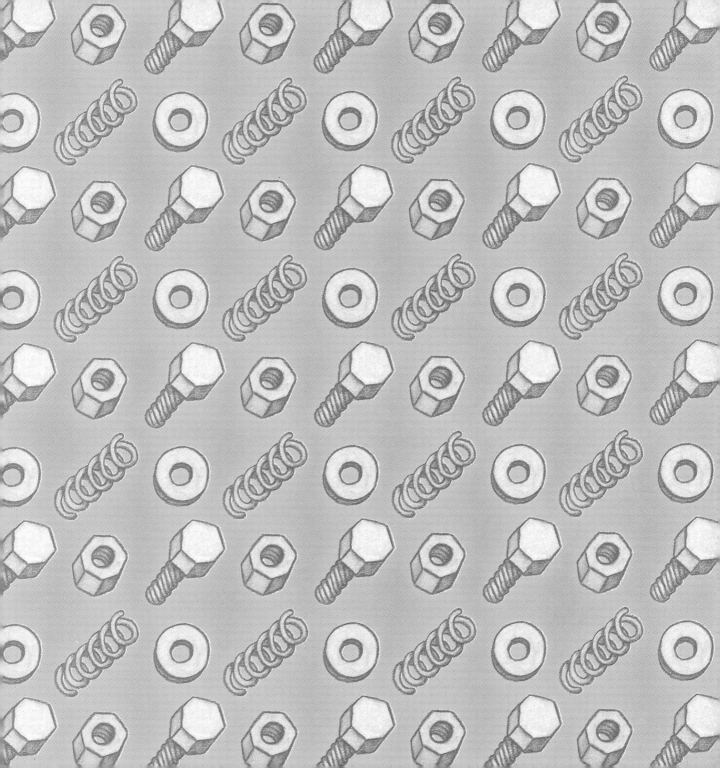

For Joseph – J.B.
For Ben – N.S.

OXFORD
UNIVERSITY PRESS

Great Clarendon Street, Oxford OX2 6DP
Oxford University Press is a department of the University of Oxford.
It furthers the University's objective of excellence in research, scholarship,
and education by publishing worldwide in

Oxford New York

Auckland Cape Town Dar es Salaam Hong Kong Karachi
Kuala Lumpur Madrid Melbourne Mexico City Nairobi
New Delhi Shanghai Taipei Toronto

With offices in

Argentina Austria Brazil Chile Czech Republic France Greece
Guatemala Hungary Italy Japan Poland Portugal Singapore
South Korea Switzerland Thailand Turkey Ukraine Vietnam

Oxford is a registered trade mark of Oxford University Press
in the UK and in certain other countries

Arrangement and selection copyright © Jill Bennett 1991
Illustrations copyright © Nick Sharratt 1991

The moral rights of the author and illustrator have been asserted

Database right Oxford University Press (maker)

First published 1991
This paperback edition 2007

British Library Cataloguing in Publication Data available

ISBN: 978-0-19-276343-3

10 9 8 7 6 5 4 3

Printed in China by Printplus

Paper used in the production of this book is a natural,
recyclable product made from wood grown in sustainable forests.
The manufacturing process conforms to the environmental
regulations of the country of origin.

Acknowledgements
The editor and publisher are grateful for permission to include the
following copyright material.

Dorothy Baruch, 'Funny the way different cars start' and 'Different
bicycles' reprinted from *I Like Machinery* by Dorothy Baruch (Harper, NY,
1933). Copyright Dorothy Baruch.** Charles Causley, 'I Love My Darling
Tractor' reprinted from *Early In The Morning* (Viking Kestrel, 1986) by
permission of David Higham Associates Ltd. Anne English, 'Washing Day'
copyright Anne English, reprinted from *Sit On the Roof and Holler*, ed.
Adrian Rumble (Bell & Hyman).** John Foster, 'Our Friend the Central
Heating' reprinted from *Things That Go*, ed. Tony Bradman (Blackie, 1989)
by permission of the author. Robert Heidbreder, 'Little Robot' and
'Rockets' reprinted from *Don't Eat Spiders*, poems © Robert Heidbreder
1985, by permission of Oxford University Press, Canada. Barbara Ireson.
'U.F.O.' reprinted from *Spaceman, Spaceman* (Transworld), by permission
of the author. Leland B Jacobs, 'The Underground Train' reprinted from
Somewhere Always Far Away?, © 1967 by Leland B Jacobs, by permission of
Henry Holt and Company, Inc. Anne Le Roy, 'The New Phone' reprinted
from *Big Dipper*, ed. June Epstein et al (OUP Australia, 1981) by
permission of the author. Marion Lines, 'Car Breakers', © Marion Lines,
reprinted from *Tower Blocks*, by kind permission of Franklin Watts.
Kit Wright, 'Cleaning Ladies' reprinted from *Hit Dog And Other Poems*
(Viking Kestrel, 1981) © Kit Wright 1981, by permission of Penguin
Books Ltd.

We have tried to secure copyright permission prior to publication but in
the case of the entries marked ** this has not been possible. If notified,
the publisher wil be pleased to include full acknowledgement at the
earliest opportunity.

MACHINE POEMS

Collected by Jill Bennett

Illustrated by Nick Sharratt

OXFORD

UNIVERSITY PRESS

I love my darling tractor

I love my darling tractor,
I love its merry din,
Its muscles made of iron and steel,
Its red and yellow skin.

I love to watch its wheels go round
However hard the day,
And from its bed inside the shed
It never thinks to stray.

It saves my arm, it saves my leg,
It saves my back from toil,
And it's merry as a skink when I give it a drink
Of water and diesel oil.

I love my darling tractor
As you can clearly see,
And so, the jolly farmer said,
Would you if you were me.

Charles Causley

Washing day

A washing machine
A sploshing machine
Splish, splash, splosh.
Whenever I use my washing machine
It splishes and splashes
All over the floor,
It splashes and sploshes
As far as the door.
I get into muddles
And step into puddles,
I don't think I'll use it
Any more.

Anne English

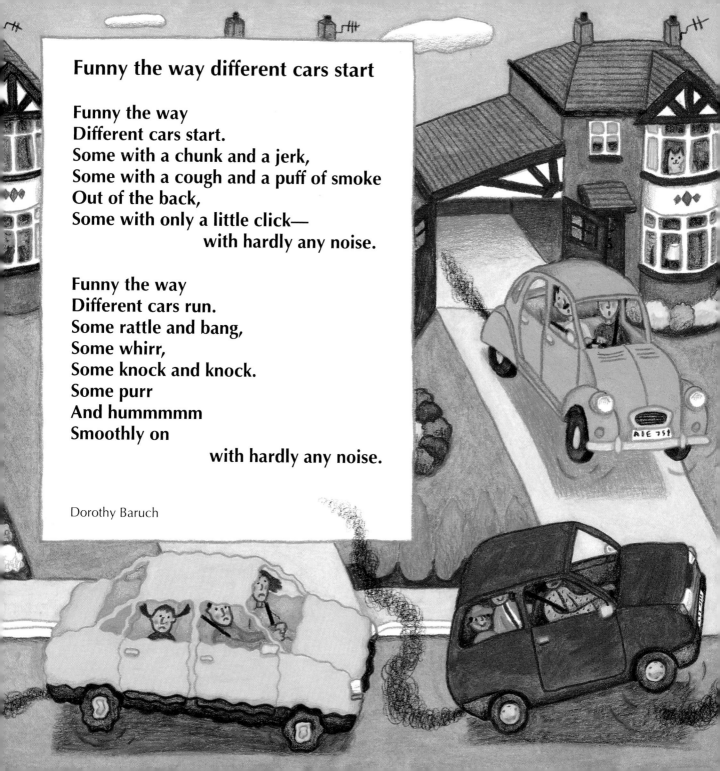

Funny the way different cars start

Funny the way
Different cars start.
Some with a chunk and a jerk,
Some with a cough and a puff of smoke
Out of the back,
Some with only a little click—
                with hardly any noise.

Funny the way
Different cars run.
Some rattle and bang,
Some whirr,
Some knock and knock.
Some purr
And hummmmm
Smoothly on
                with hardly any noise.

Dorothy Baruch

The underground train

The underground train, the
    underground train,
If you'll permit me to explain,
Is like a busy beetle black
That scoots along a silver track;
And, whether it be night or day,
The beetle has to light its way,
Because the only place it's
    found
Is deep, deep, deep, deep under-
    ground.

Leland B. Jacobs

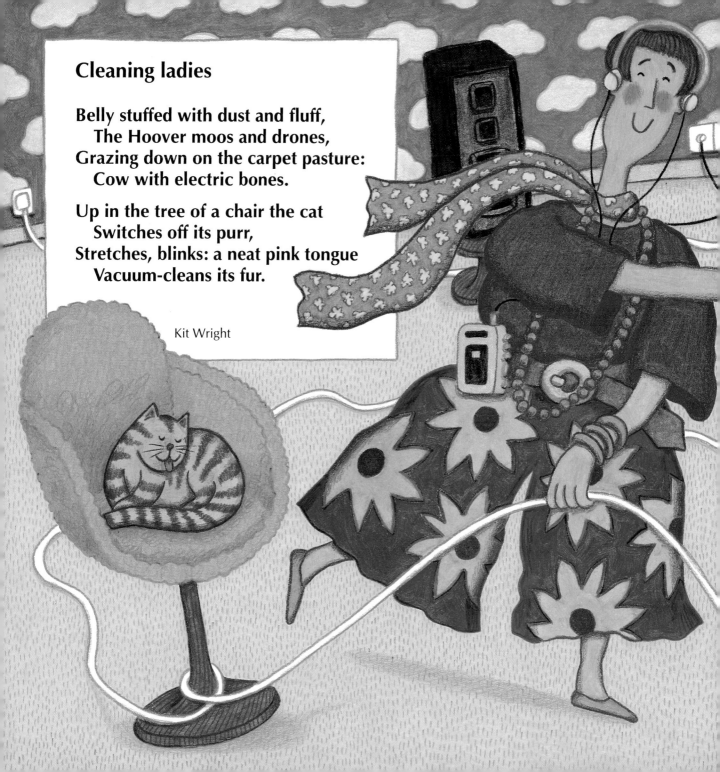

Cleaning ladies

Belly stuffed with dust and fluff,
   The Hoover moos and drones,
Grazing down on the carpet pasture:
   Cow with electric bones.

Up in the tree of a chair the cat
   Switches off its purr,
Stretches, blinks: a neat pink tongue
   Vacuum-cleans its fur.

Kit Wright

The new phone

We've got this new green phone, you see,
And all day long my friends call me,
And I just can't get on with things
Because it rings and rings and rings.

Anne LeRoy

Different bicycles

When I ride my bicycle
I pedal and pedal
Knees up, knees down.
Knees up, knees down.

But when the boy next door
Rides his.
It's whizz —
A chuck   a chuck —

And away
He's gone
With his
Knees steady-straight
In one place. . .
Because —
    His bicycle has
    A motor fastened on.

Dorothy Baruch

Little Robot

I'm a Little Robot,
    Wires make me talk.
I'm a Little Robot,
    Wires make me walk.
I'm a Little Robot,
    Wires bend my knees.
I'm a Little Robot,
    Wires make me sneeze.
        AAAACHOOOOOO!

I'm a Little Robot,
    Wires make me work.
So if you ever cross them,
    I'll probably go BERSERK!

ZOING ZOING BOINK!
ZOING ZOING BOINK!
ZING!

Robert Heidbreder

Car breakers

There's a graveyard in our street,
But it's not for putting people in;
The bodies they bury here
Are made of steel and paint and tin.

The people come and leave their wrecks
For crunching in the giant jaws
Of a great hungry car-machine,
That lives on bonnets, wheels and doors.

When I pass by the yard at night,
I sometimes think I hear a sound
Of ghostly horns that moan and whine,
Upon that metal-graveyard mound.

Marion Lines

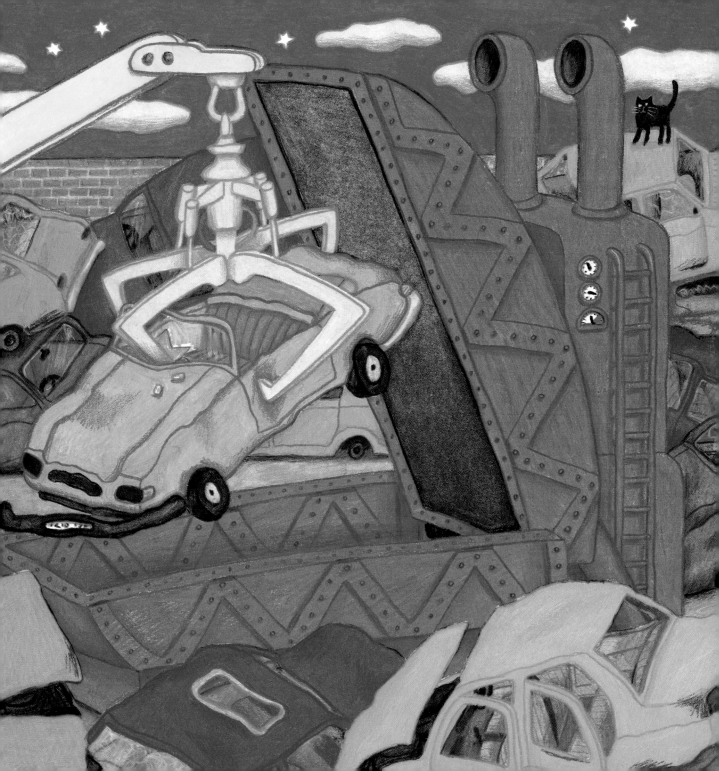

Our friend the central heating

There's a monster in our house —
Our friend the central heating.
From the way its stomach rumbles,
Goodness knows what it's been eating!

It wakes us up at night-time
With its gurglings and its groanings,
Its clatterings and its clanging,
Its mutterings and moanings.

Mum says it lives on water,
In answer to my question.
I think that it must gulp it down
To get such indigestion!

John Foster

Rockets

Rockets flying out in space,
Rockets flying every place,
Rockets from Earth
        to Venus and Mars,
        to silver moons and shining stars,
Rockets to galaxies far away,
I think I'll build a rocket some day.
I'll fuel it first.
I'll fly it away.
I'll land in time for Christmas day,
On Pluto, Neptune, Saturn or Mars,
On a silver moon
Or a shining star.

Robert Heidbreder

U.F.O.

Hear that humming. . .
Spaceship's coming.

       Watch that light. . .
       It's shining bright.

Feel that air. . .
It's landing there.

       Hear that roar. . .
       Look at the door.

See the crew. . .
They're coming through!

Barbara Ireson

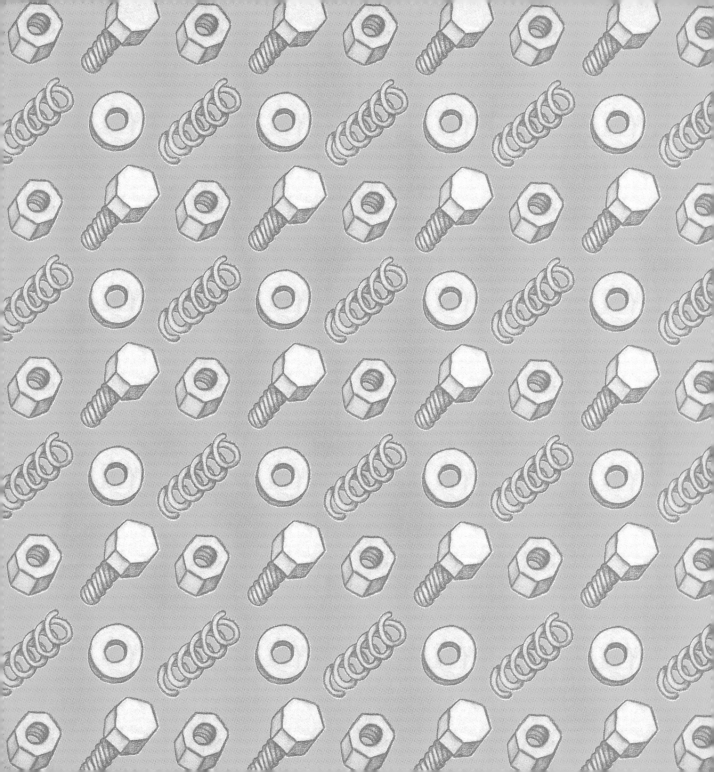

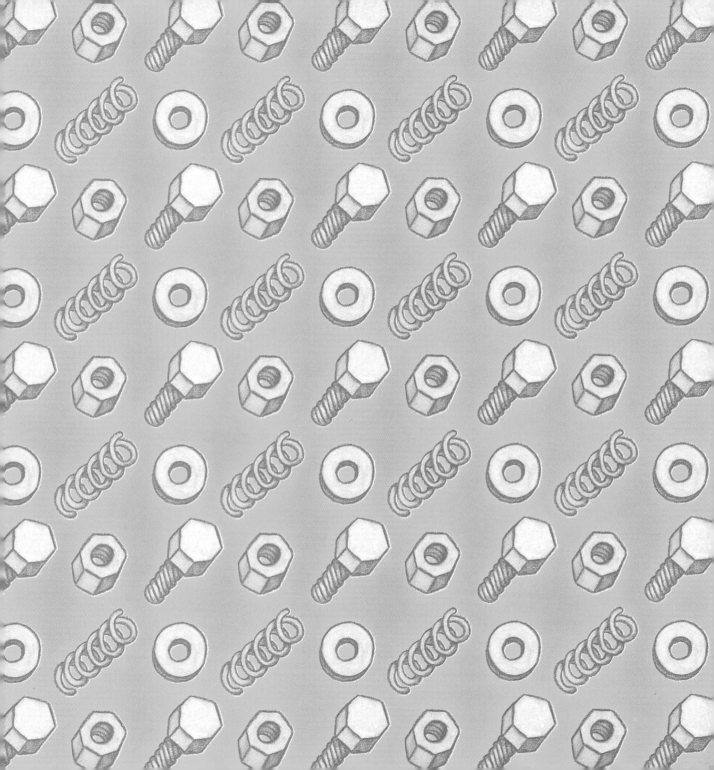